VINTAGE TRAVEL
POSTERS

VINTAGE TRAVEL
POSTERS

GOING PLACES IN STYLE

PATIENCE COSTER

ARCTURUS

ARCTURUS

This edition published in 2016 by Arcturus Publishing Limited
26/27 Bickels Yard, 151–153 Bermondsey Street,
London SE1 3HA, UK

ISBN: 978-1-78404-748-1
AD004387UK

Printed in China

Contents

From Grand Tour to Package Trip

The history of travel posters is bound up with the history of modern transportation – of railways and ocean liners, the motorcar and the passenger plane. In relative terms it is fairly brief, dating from 1870, when the printing industry perfected colour lithography and made mass production possible. Writing in 1973, poster expert John Barnicoat says: 'In little more than a hundred years, it [the poster] has come to be recognized as a vital art form, attracting artists at every level, from painters to theatrical and commercial designers.'

Tourism in the Ancient World

Although the poster itself is a recent invention, the practice of travelling for pleasure, health and self-improvement dates back thousands of years. Today's lucrative global tourism industry originated as the hobby of an elite minority pursuing a luxury lifestyle. In Ancient Egypt, under the pharaohs, groups representing the cream of society visited monuments and relics; similarly Ancient Greeks journeyed to visit the Oracle at Delphi and take part in the Olympic Games.

Later, the Romans developed an infrastructure of roads through Europe and North Africa, which not only facilitated the movement of troops and supplies but also paved the way for private voyages. By the 1st century AD, wealthy citizens were taking their holidays at thermal baths in various fancy resorts and, like millions of

ABOVE: A travel poster from 1896 by Henri de Toulouse-Lautrec.

FACING PAGE: In this 19th-century painting, artist Emil Brack shows a wealthy young man regaling his sweetheart with plans for his Grand Tour.

tourists today, sunning themselves on the beaches of Egypt and Greece. Following the fall of the Roman Empire, the condition of roads and the practice of travelling for pleasure went into decline. During the Middle Ages travel abroad existed just for a select few – mainly in the form of pilgrimage or for educational improvement – and was dangerous, arduous and fraught with complications.

The Grand Tour

In the 16th century the idea grew up of journeying as a way of achieving self-realization or obtaining training as a craftsman. This notion transmuted into the Grand Tour, an extended trek round the cultural sites of Europe undertaken by wealthy young men to broaden their education and burnish their social graces. After university they would embark on a tour of Germany, France and Italy, generally for a period of between one and three years. Needless to say, these Grand Tours involved extensive planning and an entourage of domestic staff. As well as the classical sites, cities such as London, Amsterdam, Munich, Vienna and Prague with their royal courts and aristocratic estates were popular destinations.

Thomas Cook & Son

In the late 1700s, the birth of the Industrial Revolution in Britain saw the creation of a moneyed manufacturing class, which meant tourism was no longer confined to the aristocracy. By the middle of the 1800s, railways had opened up across Europe (although they would not widely be used by tourists until the mountain railway became popular

ABOVE: A Works Progress Administration (WPA) poster from the 1940s, designed to inspire American citizens to explore their beautiful homeland.

at the end of the century). In 1841, Thomas Cook, a Baptist minister from Market Harborough, a small town in England, arranged for the new Midland Counties Railway to take a group of temperance campaigners from Leicester to a rally in Loughborough. Within a few years he had started his own company, running trips for pleasure and taking a percentage of the price of tickets sold. Business grew and by the 1850s Cook was conducting 'grand circular tours' of Europe. The 1860s found him taking parties to Egypt and the United States, charging a fixed rate for travel, food and accommodation. In 1872, he formed a partnership with his commercially minded son, John, naming the travel agency Thomas Cook & Son, with offices in Fleet Street, London. The phrase 'Cook's Tours' soon became shorthand for guided holidays where the customer's needs were catered for and the itinerary carefully planned.

Transportation revolution

The 19th-century explosion of new travel options resulted in short-stay excursions becoming popular. And although this revolution did not filter through to the mass of ordinary working people, it certainly benefitted the newly established middle classes who were keen to experience the glamour of foreign travel. Equipped with guides such as *Bradshaw's, Baedeker's* or *Murray's Handbook*, this legion of sightseers, determined to track down the sites essential to their spiritual and social development, travelled far afield for the first time. Meanwhile, holidays for the working classes were restricted to day trips. It would be another hundred years before poorer people experienced the delights of an extended break, either at home or abroad.

In 1812, steam navigation began in Scotland and spread swiftly throughout Europe. Although the first purpose-built passenger ships were not launched until around 1900, the Mediterranean or transatlantic cruise became bywords for glamour and luxury soon after that date. (This image, however, would encounter a serious setback when state-of-the-art ocean liner *Titanic* sank on her maiden voyage in 1912).

Winter tourism

The fashion for winter tourism began in St Moritz, Switzerland in 1864, when hotel manager Johannes Badrutt invited a group of summer guests to come back in winter to experience the snowy landscape. He promised that if they didn't enjoy themselves he would bear the cost of their return journey from London. The dry, clear mountain air, sunny weather and majestic landscape witnessed by this first group of winter tourists started a trend for healthy outdoor-pursuit holidays that continues to this day.

In the early 1900s the invention of the motorcar gave tourists greater independence and increased the scope of destinations available to them. There was a tourism boom, with rail networks, steamship companies and, eventually, airlines competing ferociously to sell their services. But behind the hard-nosed commercialism an art form was flowering. The travel poster reflected significant trends in art, design and fashion, as well as social and cultural developments in general. Like other forms of advertising, it exuded colour, excitement and glamour together with the promise of a transformative experience that would relieve the monotony of humdrum, everyday human life. Even towards the end of the 20th century, by which time television advertising and the internet had largely taken over from the printed medium, travel posters continued to have a vintage feel, harking back to an era of debonaire men, soignée women, open-topped sports cars and fluttering scarves.

This book features some of the brightest and most beautiful posters of the late-19th to mid-20th centuries, encompassing the romantic visions and passing fancies that constitute much of human aspiration – a shimmering illusion of life in the fast lane.

Patience Coster

ABOVE: This advert for the 1988 Monaco Grand Prix pays homage to the Art Deco heyday of the travel poster.

The Gilded Age

Towards the end of the 19th century, the Belle Époque's colourful spirit was evident in travel posters depicting a carefree, sunny world. Born out of a period of peace and stability, and confidence in the potential of new technologies to liberate people from lives of toil and drudgery, this optimism was the essence of what seemed to be a gilded age.

In reality, only holidaymakers from the upper and middle classes could afford to travel far afield, and they did so initially for cultural or health reasons. But as railways and international cruise lines carried visitors to increasingly exotic locations, new pleasures beckoned. The fashionable could be seen promenading along seafront boulevards, showing off their clothes; and gambling resorts were a magnet for those who felt their lives lacked excitement. Travel companies quickly seized on this mood of hedonism, commissioning artists such as Alphonse Mucha to apply their Art Nouveau styling to posters advertising the delights of the Côte d'Azur and other racy, glamorous destinations.

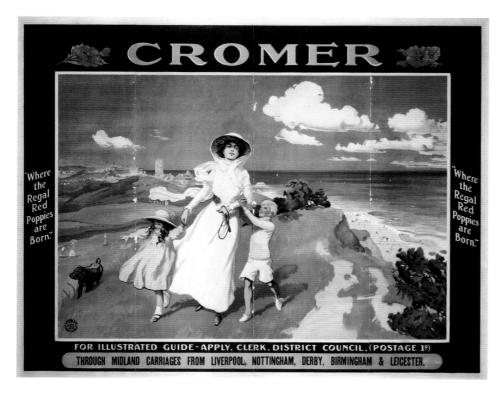

LEFT: In a poster from 1900 produced by the Midland Railway and Cromer District Council, an elegantly dressed woman takes her children and dog for a coastal walk in Norfolk.

RIGHT: A Uganda Railway poster from 1908 shows the track between the Kenyan cities of Nairobi and Mombasa. Communication links were vital to the administration of British colonies in Africa and elsewhere.

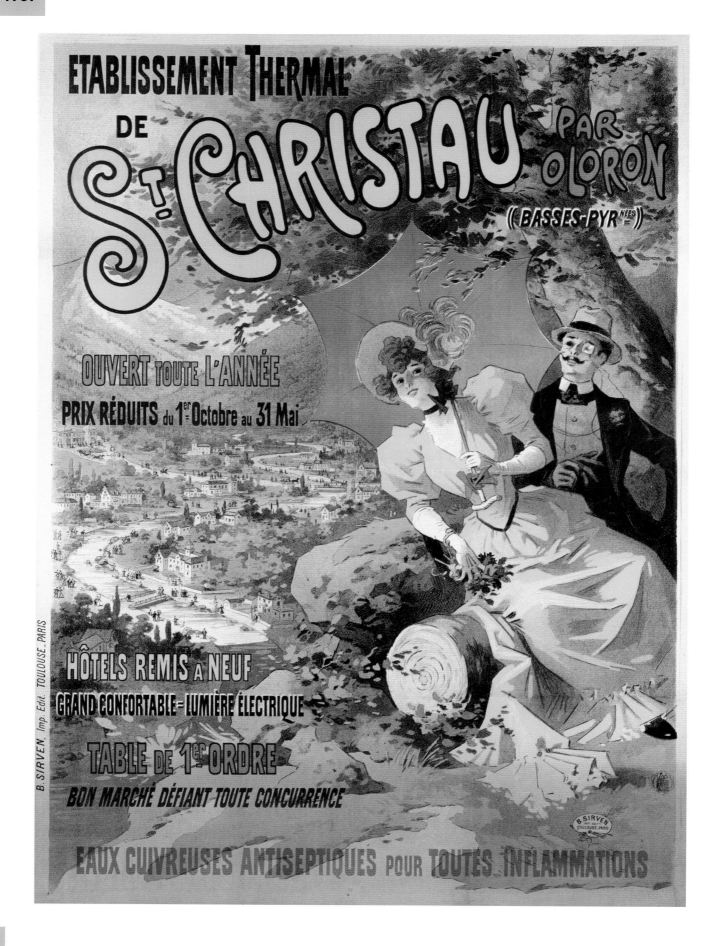

ABOVE: The funicular railway built in 1892 to carry visitors up the cliff to the basilica of Notre-Dame de la Garde, a neo-Byzantine church built at the highest point in Marseille, was an instant hit with tourists. But a few decades later the advent of the automobile put paid to its popularity. It was demolished in the 1960s after transporting 20 million passengers over 75 years.

ABOVE: Passenger ships catered for wealthy travellers by providing luxurious spaces at sea equal to the finest hotels and restaurants. The Deutsche Ost-Afrika Linie (German East Africa Line) was a shipping company established in 1890 to compete in a market dominated by the British. In this poster, a boat full of admiring onlookers pays due deference to the showpiece 'ship of state'.

FACING PAGE: In the early 1900s, the dominant motif of travelling and holidaying was recuperation. The hotel of St Christau near Oloron-Sante-Marie in the French Pyrenees boasts electric lights, first-class dining and antiseptic waters to cure all ills – everything the well-heeled tourist could wish for…

MONACO · MONTE-CARLO

FACING PAGE: A French advertisement for Cycles Terrot from around 1900 shows a nonchalant young woman riding her bicycle on a railway track, seemingly unconcerned by the presence of an oncoming train!

ABOVE: Czech artist Alphonse Mucha was the pre-eminent exponent of French Art Nouveau. This 1897 travel poster is a classic example of his style.

The American Line, founded in 1871 as part of the Pennsylvania Railroad, was the biggest US shipping line of its time, handling traffic between Philadelphia and New York City and the British ports of Liverpool and Southampton. It owned the largest steamship pier in New York, which was fitted with a second storey so that passengers and freight could be kept separate on embarkation and landing.

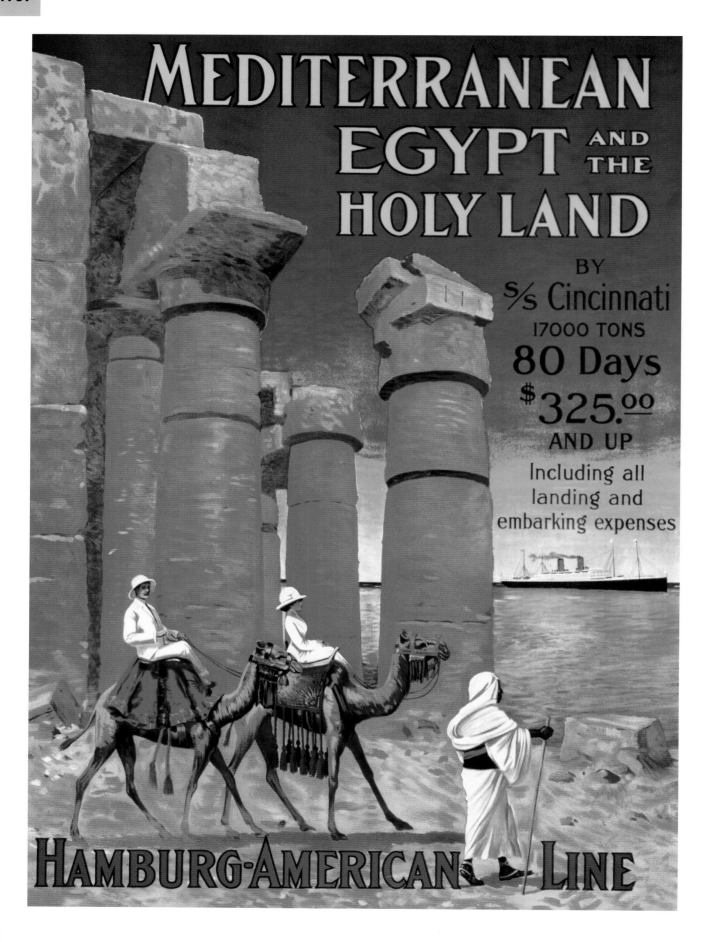

FACING PAGE: A 1909 poster for the Hamburg-American Line, the first German transatlantic steamship company, reflects the Western fascination with ancient sites.

ABOVE: The Orient Express was a 'lightning luxury' passenger train service established in 1883 by a Belgian banker's son. Its original route was from Paris to Constantinople (now Istanbul).

LEFT: Relaxed, stylish travelling on the Chicago and Alton Railroad, around 1890.

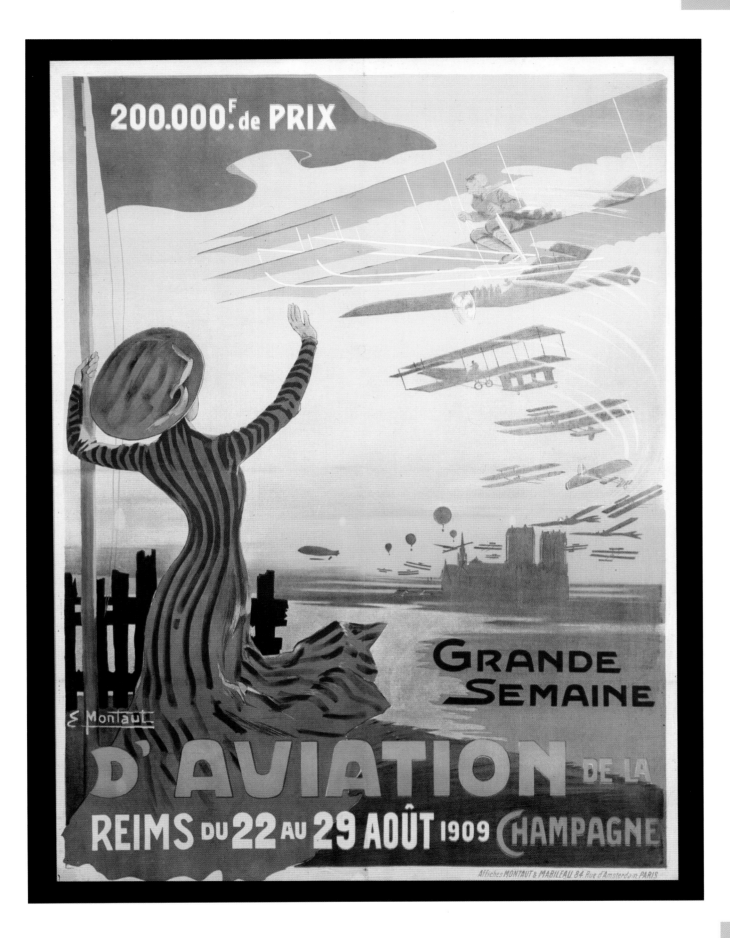

Pack Up Your Troubles

In the years immediately preceding World War I, European tourism was a growth industry. Trips to fashionable watering holes and gambling resorts in countries such as Belgium, France, Switzerland, Germany and Italy remained popular. But in 1914, declaration of war meant all notions of frivolity and pleasure were brutally swept aside and tourism stagnated.

With travel to Europe no longer advisable, Americans looked for recreation closer to home. In 1910, the establishment of the Glacier National Park in Montana saw the start of domestic tourism in the United States. Spurred on by the development of the Great Northern Railroad, this park helped launch 'See America First', a campaign aimed at wealthy East Coast Americans who had previously spent the collective sum of $500 million a year visiting Europe.

LEFT: The banking operation Wells Fargo & Co. set up a stagecoach delivery service in the 1860s. Following the completion of the transcontinental railroad in 1869 it became America's first nationwide express company. This poster dates from 1915.

FACING PAGE: A poster inviting visitors to an arts and crafts exhibition in Malmö, by Swedish artist and author Ernst Norlind.

FACING PAGE: This cutaway view of RMS *Aquitania* from around 1912 shows the amenities and luxurious accommodation on board the Cunard Line vessel.

ABOVE: The first round-the-world cruise took place in 1881, when the P&O liner SS *Ceylon* set out from Liverpool, England. In 1910, the Hamburg American Line's steam-powered SS *Cleveland* began a 110-day circumnavigation of the globe. Thousands of people thronged to the docks in San Francisco to watch the liner depart on its 24,000-mile voyage. This 1912 poster suggests that business continued to boom right up to the outbreak of war.

ABOVE: The unified state ownership of Belgian railways brought considerable advantages for the tourism industry. It facilitated the nationwide marketing of resorts, unencumbered by the problems arising from the fragmented pattern of railway ownership in countries such as Britain. By 1910, advertisements for various watering places appeared regularly in international tourist journals.

RIGHT: A stunning view of Amalfi, from a series of posters featuring the Italian coastline by Mario Borgoni, painted around 1915.

OLYMPIC GAMES
↷ STOCKHOLM 1912 ↶
JUNE 29 th — JULY 22 nd.

A. BÖRTZELLS TR. A. B. STOCKHOLM

ABOVE: The 1912 Summer Olympic Games in Stockholm were the last to issue solid gold medals, but the first to feature art competitions, women's diving and swimming, and decathlon and pentathlon events.

FACING PAGE: This Dutch poster by Jan Willem Sluiter shows a fashionable couple on the French Riviera. Produced on the eve of the Great War, brimming with optimism and innovation, it illustrates how quickly our certainties can be swept away.

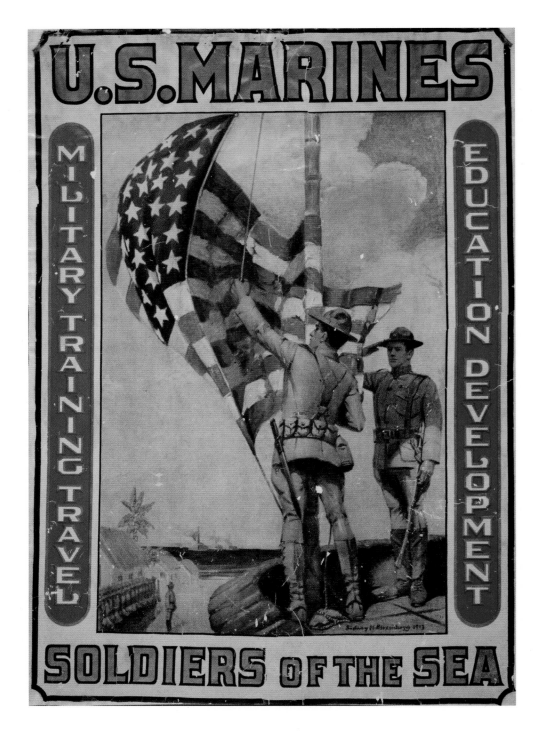

ABOVE: A 1913 poster shows US Marines raising an American flag and emphasizes the rich variety of life as a new recruit. As travel was very expensive at that time, the opportunity to see different parts of the world was a huge selling point for young Americans; joining the US Marine corps was a way of doing this while being paid.

FACING PAGE: This beautiful Italian Tourist Board poster from 1920 by Vittorio Grassi captures the quality of Venetian light and the way in which it plays upon the surface of the lagoon. This poster was published in several languages – a reflection of Italy's booming tourist industry.

ABOVE: With the cycling craze as its theme, this poster by French illustrator and caricaturist Mich (Jean-Marie-Michel Liébaux) shows a happy hobo on his old-fashioned unicycle fitted with the latest go-faster tyre.

ABOVE: The growth of Thomas Cook & Son (see pages 7–8) was consolidated by Thomas' son, John Mason Cook. By 1888 the company had established offices around the world. This poster dates from 1910.

ABOVE: The Pera Palace hotel in Constantinople was built in 1892 to provide accommodation for passengers on the Orient Express.

FACING PAGE: The Bangor and Aroostook Railroad in Maine was originally set up to haul potatoes, coal and timber. During World War I, its small fleet of passenger trains was put to good use by Americans holidaying at home.

LEFT: Perhaps in response to the copywriter's laboured efforts, an Edwardian bathing beauty clings wanly to a buoy in this poster for South Eastern & Chatham Railway, promoting travel to the Kent resort of Deal.

RIGHT: Setting out on holiday or to a new life? This post-World War I British advertisement for Cunard Line travel to Canada is suffused with soft golden light, promising a bright dawn for the young adventurers.

We're In the Money

In the Roaring Twenties money flowed, the rich let their hair down and partied and international air travel took off. After World War I, the victorious Allies divided the spoils, including Germany's colonies, among themselves. The 1920s and 1930s marked the apex of these European empires. Despite increasing signs of unrest and even revolt, wealthy tourists regarded them as exotic playgrounds.

Meanwhile, closer to home, the seaside remained a much-loved destination. And while winter sports were still the preserve of the rich, for the less well-off, adventure holidays such as the summer retreat became popular. These healthy, economical vacations were inspired by love of the countryside and a desire to escape the city's grime and bustle. Holidaymakers immersed themselves in the beauty and grandeur of the natural world, and walking trails and guest houses were set up to cater for their needs. Communing with nature in this way must have been therapeutic following the trauma of the war years.

LMS LONDON
BY CHARLES SIMS. R.A.

LEFT: In the 1920s a global financial boom made England's capital city a desirable destination for people who wanted to get rich quick. Charles Sims' poster for London Midland & Scottish Railway shows a strange creature scattering bags of money while various characters step over one another to collect it.

FACING PAGE: A 1924 Winter Olympics poster by French artist Roger Soubie, who would go on to design around 2,000 movie posters, including several for Elvis Presley.

RIGHT: An atmospheric poster of a moonlit street painted in a limited palette of colours by Henry George Gawthorn for India State Railways Bureau in 1920. Gawthorn originally trained as an architect, but later turned to graphic design, producing posters for the London & North Eastern Railway, among others.

A STREET BY MOONLIGHT

VISIT INDIA

APPLY
India
STATE RAILWAYS
BUREAU

DELHI HOUSE
38 EAST 57th STREET
NEW YORK

ADAMS BROS. & SHARDLOW. LTD. LONDON.

FACING PAGE: Children on board a steamship wave a fan decorated with the sun-disc symbol of the Japanese flag.

EGYPTIAN STATE RAILWAYS

KARNAK

LEFT: Occupied by Britain from 1882 to 1922, Egypt was a popular winter destination for wealthy tourists despite the fact that tensions often ran high between the two countries. The significance of the overland route from Europe through Egypt to India and the East had undoubtedly influenced the construction of a railway along the Nile Valley in the 19th century. Between 1925 and 1932 the track, which had been badly damaged during World War I, underwent extensive renewal.

ABOVE: The French railway company PLM mainly linked the southeast of the country with Mediterranean destinations. This poster from 1920 by Géo Dorival shows the Roman Forum at dawn.

ABOVE: The bold, stringent Art Deco designs of Ukrainian-born Cassandre (Adolphe-Jean-Marie Mouron) greatly influenced advertising art in the first half of the 20th century.

FACING PAGE: Cassandre's dynamic 1927 poster for Étoile du Nord, the Paris to Amsterdam express train, was designed to convey (and be read at) speed.

RIGHT: A Handley Page W10 biplane traverses a map of Europe. Imperial Airways Limited was formed following the merger of four existing airlines and operated from 1924 to 1939, serving parts of Europe but principally the British Empire routes to India, South Africa and the Far East. The aircraft were small, most seating fewer than 20 passengers.

RIGHT: Another Art Deco marvel, produced for the London & North Eastern Railway to advertise their day and night ferry service to Germany from the North Sea port of Harwich in Essex. The blue and pink theme was a favourite of artist Ladislas Freiwirth.

What to see in AUSTRIA

PRINTED IN AUSTRIA

ISSUED BY THE
„ÖSTERREICHISCHE VERKEHRSWERBUNG"
AUSTRIAN FEDERAL RAILWAYS, VIENNA

ABOVE: Newly liberated, independent, well-heeled 1920s women looked and behaved very differently from their predecessors, as illustrated by this Austrian Railways poster.

ABOVE: Aviation pioneer Glenn Curtiss' flying service operated from 1929 on two routes out of Boston to Nantucket and Bangor, but by 1932 his company had folded.

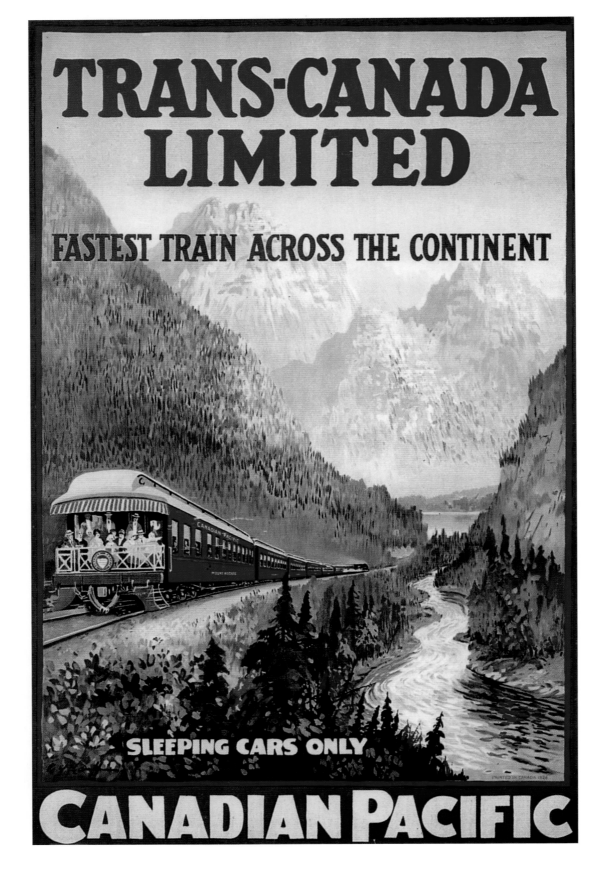

ABOVE: Canadian Pacific Railway's Trans-Canada Limited was a luxury passenger train. G.Y. Kauffman's poster for this 'hotel on wheels' dates from 1924.

LEFT: A colourful, Western-stylized Fourth of July parade scene by Edward V. Brewer, an American illustrator best known for his Cream of Wheat advertising work. With his folksy style, Brewer, from St Paul, was known as Minnesota's answer to Norman Rockwell. This poster was used by the Northern Pacific Railroad to encourage tourists to visit the Rocky Mountains.

RIGHT: This 1929 poster was Leslie Ragan's first for New York Central Lines, the company for whom he would produce many of his iconic Art Deco images. With its depth of field and combination of shadowy and luminous areas, this view of Chicago's Michigan Avenue skyscrapers under a towering thunderhead evokes the romance and grandeur of a midwestern Athens. Iowa-born Ragan was influenced by the American illustrative tradition of N.C. Wyeth and Maxfield Parrish.

LONDON'S TRAMWAYS

CHRISTMAS SHOPPING
TAKE AN ALL-DAY
1/- TICKET

LEFT: In 1926, fashion-conscious young women get their Christmas shopping done in style – by tram.

RIGHT: In the same year, the talents of pastoralist Ethelbert White were deployed by Southern Electric Railways to promote the rural idyll of life in Kent.

LIVE IN KENT
AND BE CONTENT.
FREQUENT ELECTRIC TRAINS DAY AND NIGHT.
"THE COUNTRY AT LONDON'S DOOR,"
FREE AT ANY S.R. ENQUIRY OFFICE.

SOUTHERN RAILWAY ADVERTISING.   H. A. WALKER,   GENERAL MANAGER.

Above: In the summer, wealthy families from Lille and Paris would decamp to Wimereux on the north coast of France, where many of them had second homes. This stylized, Art Deco railway poster by Leon Dupin highlights the resort's many attractions, including golf, tennis, horse racing and gambling.

RIGHT: This poster by British artist Frank Newbould for the White Star Line shows the RMS *Olympic* (a sister ship to the *Titanic*) in New York harbour. In the background is the Woolworth Building which was the world's tallest building at the time. Newbould's posters were characterized by the use of strong shapes and colours.

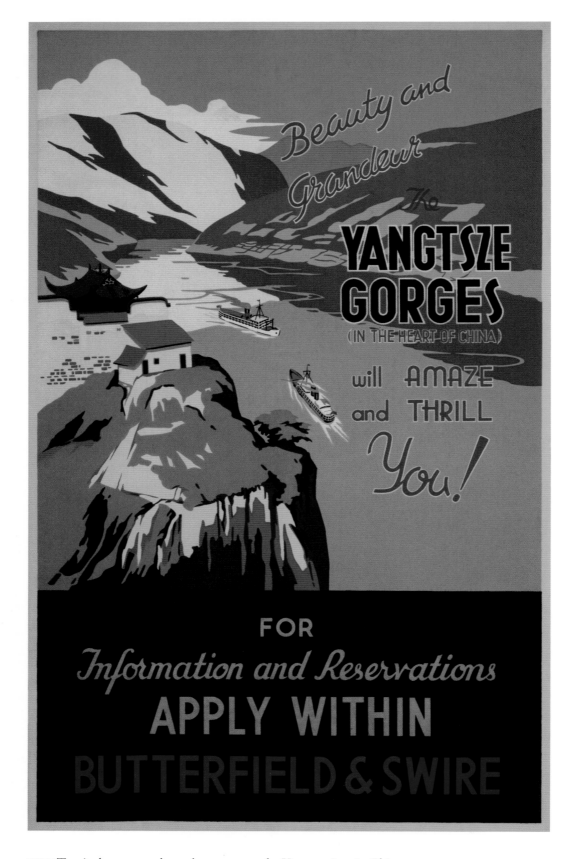

RIGHT: Tourist boats pass through a gorge on the Yangtze river in China. Originally an import-export company operating out of Liverpool, Butterfield & Swire established Shanghai and Hong Kong offices in the 1860s.

ABOVE: A 1924 poster by Severino Trematore. Arrested in London during World War II, the artist died while being deported to Canada when his ship was torpedoed in the Atlantic.

Tourism For the Masses

During the 1930s travel posters reached their artistic zenith. In Italy, the influence of Futurism, with its forceful images, filtered through to the commercial sector. Elsewhere the exuberance and confidence of Art Deco endorsed the rapid industrialization that was taking place.

But the buoyant mood depicted by poster designers could not conceal the fact that the world was gripped by a severe economic recession. With many of the wealthy suddenly bankrupt, who now could afford to splash out on luxuries such as holidays? In Germany, inexpensive walking tours and cruises that included accommodation and meals were offered to people on average incomes. In the United States, unemployed young men were given conservation work in parks and forests. Between 1930 and 1939 the US government pumped money into the national parks system and visitor numbers more than quadrupled.

SEE AMERICA
UNITED STATES TRAVEL BUREAU

MADE BY WORKS PROGRESS ADMINISTRATION · FEDERAL ART PROJECT NYC

LEFT: Despite the Great Depression, President Franklin D. Roosevelt poured money into US parks in a determined effort to bolster national confidence and get Americans to explore the great outdoors.

FACING PAGE: Franz Lenhart's Futurist vision of winter sports in Italy, 1935.

ABOVE: In 1935, the Italian term 'lido' was adopted to describe an outdoor swimming pool in London. This 1932 advertisement for Lake Lucerne Lido in Switzerland by Albert Solbach shows an androgynous woman striking a powerful pose characteristic of the time.

ABOVE: Venice Lido was a popular resort for the rich and famous. This poster for the Grand Hotel des Bains is by Filippo Romoli.

夏の三保

名古屋鐵道局

ABOVE: Splashing in the waves in the shadow of Mount Fuji; by 1936, tourist spending was Japan's fourth-largest source of foreign exchange revenue after cotton, raw silk and silk products.

FACING PAGE: A mesmerizing Art Deco poster for Japanese Government Railways by Satomi Munetsugu, 1937.

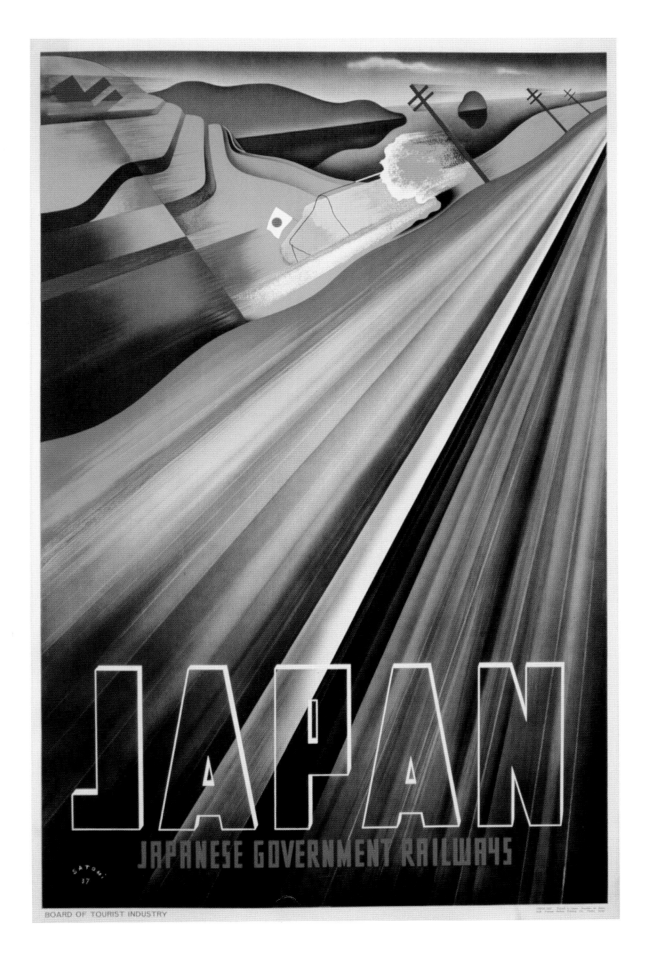

LEFT: Tourism to Australia became feasible in the 1930s with the advent of faster long-haul aviation. James Northfield created a series of striking posters for the newly established Australian National Travel Association. This classic cleverly shows the attractions both above and below the waters of the Great Barrier Reef.

RIGHT: Northfield's posters helped to promote Australia both at home and abroad. He was renowned for his skill at capturing extremes of light and shade.

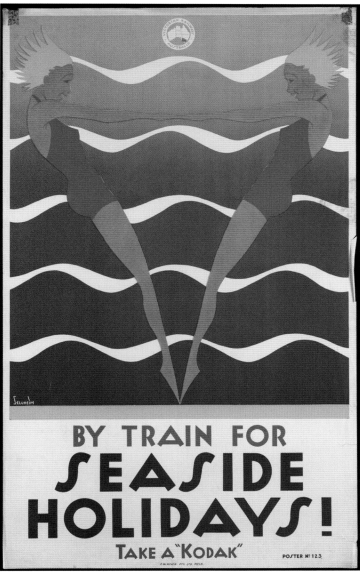

LEFT: Gert Sellheim was born in Estonia to German parents and studied architecture at universities in Germany before migrating to Western Australia in 1926. He established an architecture and design practice in Melbourne in 1930, and moved to Sydney in 1947. Sellheim's most famous design is Qantas airline's distinctive flying kangaroo logo, created in 1947.

RIGHT: Sellheim's most memorable posters were produced for the Australian National Travel Association and were widely distributed overseas to encourage tourism.

ABOVE: Alfred Booth and Co., a British trading and shipping company founded in 1866, introduced passenger cruises to South America advertising '1,000 miles up the Amazon'. It modernized its fleet with new ships in the 1920s and 1930s, but lost several in World War II.

FACING PAGE: In the 1930s, Cuba was one of the Caribbean's foremost tourist destinations.

FACING PAGE: A 1937 poster by Paul George Lawler shows a Sikorsky S-42 flying boat over Sugar Loaf mountain in Rio de Janeiro harbour, with the huge statue of Christ overlooking Botafogo Beach.

ABOVE: This 1936 tourism poster for Panama, printed in Ecuador, features a carnival queen on a float.

SEE AMERICA
WELCOME TO MONTANA
UNITED STATES TRAVEL BUREAU

USA
WORK
WPA

MADE BY WORKS PROGRESS ADMINISTRATION · FEDERAL ART PROJECT NYC

ABOVE: The preservation of wild places was often a bitterly fought battle between rival interests. In the 'See America First' campaign, the federal government portrayed the parks as national assets.

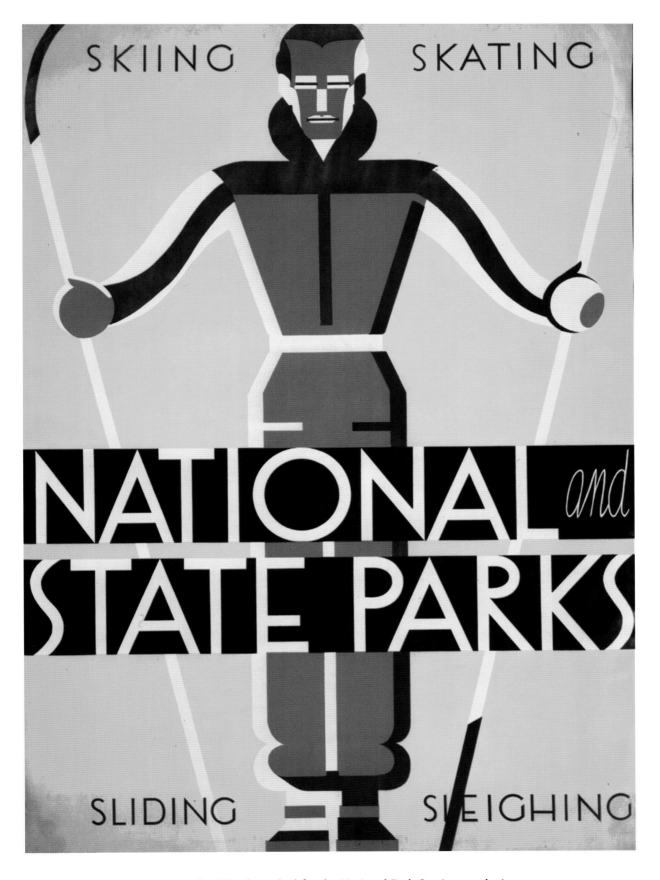

SKIING   SKATING

NATIONAL and STATE PARKS

SLIDING   SLEIGHING

ABOVE: Commercial artist Dorothy Waugh worked for the National Park Service, producing copy, layout and artwork, such as this outdoor activities poster, throughout the 1930s.

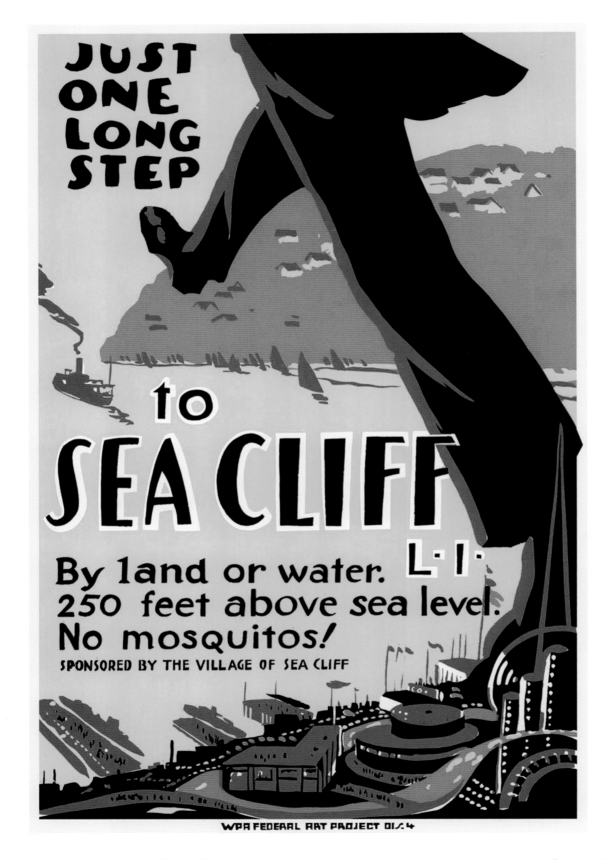

JUST ONE LONG STEP to SEA CLIFF L·I·

By land or water. 250 feet above sea level. No mosquitos!

SPONSORED BY THE VILLAGE OF SEA CLIFF

WPA FEDERAL ART PROJECT DI/: 4

ABOVE: A slightly surreal WPA Federal Art Project poster for the village of Sea Cliff, Long Island, where the absence of insect life is a selling point.

FACING PAGE: A poster from 1937 advertises cheap tours through Denmark, Finland, Norway and Sweden for families on a budget.

ABOVE: A poster advertising the Hamburg Southern Line by award-winning artist Ottomar Anton demonstrates his innovative use of colour. German-born Anton was a painter, graphic artist and university professor. He designed posters for shipping companies and the logo for the world famous eau de cologne, 4711.

Mitre Peak, Milford Sound

NEW ZEALAND

ABOVE: Designer Leonard Cornwall Mitchell worked for the New Zealand government producing posters, booklet covers, coins and over 90 stamps championing the attractions of his country.

ABOVE: A 1936 poster by Albert Fuss advertises 'North Country Trips' via the Hamburg-American Line.

ABOVE: The good old red, white and blue … a tourism
brochure for London by John Farleigh, 1936.

ABOVE: A view of Dover by British painter and graphic artist
Leonard Richmond in a *plein air* style influenced by the St Ives
Art Colony, of which he was a member at this time.

ABOVE: A 1932 advert for the Holland America shipping line celebrates the new age in its dynamic, confident Art Deco design.

FACING PAGE: This 1937 poster by Austrian commercial artist Arthur Zelger advertises Alpine skiing in the Tyrol where, by 1930, a thriving winter tourism industry had developed.

ABOVE: A stunning 1937 poster by British self-confessed 'master craftsman' Tom Purvis, one of the greatest commercial artists of his generation. In the words of a contemporary, Bert Thomas: 'His posters were the finest that ever appeared on the hoardings. They were real posters, not just showcards enlarged, as most posters were in those days. One could take them in at a glance while passing on a bus, which is the test of a good poster.'

ABOVE: Air travel in the 1930s tended to be work-related – businessmen, officials and engineers accounted for most passengers, as shown in this 1936 poster.

ABOVE: A flamenco dancer is used to promote the Spring Festival in Seville, Spain.

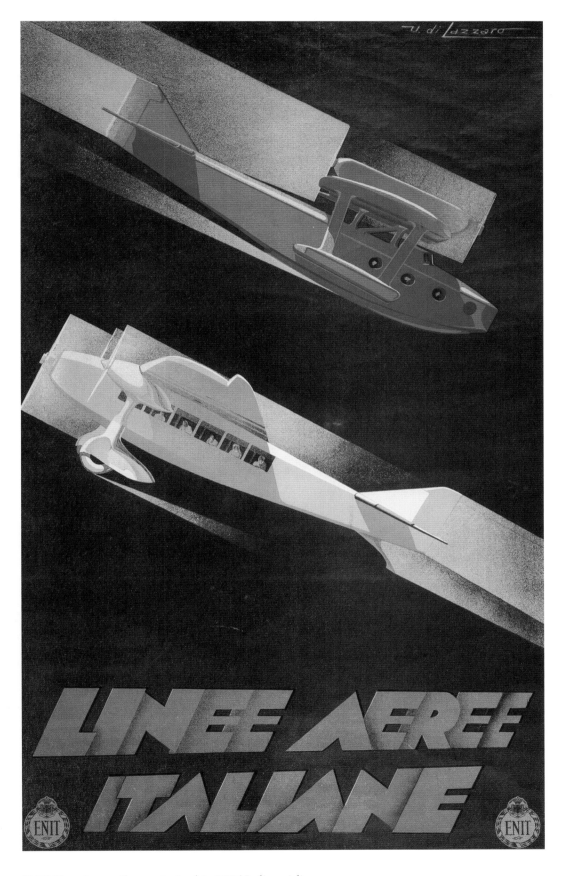

ABOVE: Futurism strikes again in this 1936 Italian airline poster by Umberto di Lazzaro.

LEFT: In 1932, Herbert Matter's pioneering travel posters for the Swiss National Tourist Office were the first to use photography as collage. Photographer and designer Matter had worked with Cassandre on poster design and with the legendary urban planner Le Corbusier on architecture and displays in Paris.

RIGHT: Another example of Herbert Matter's photomontage technique achieved by manipulation of the negative, retouching, cropping, cutting out and enlarging.

FAR RIGHT: Cassandre created this image to promote travel on the famous ocean liner *Normandie*. It has since become an icon of 20th century Art Deco and Modernist poster design.

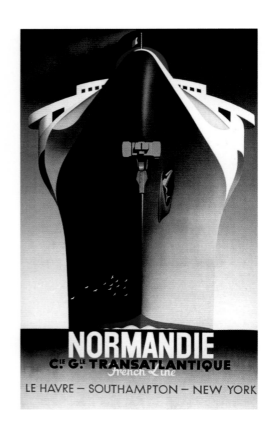

ABOVE: A 1939 poster by Danish artist and scenery painter Helge Refn.

ABOVE: Founded in 1926 by Joseph Stalin, Intourist was the official state travel agency of the Soviet Union. It grew into one of the largest tourism organizations in the world, with a network embracing banks, hotels and bureaux de change.

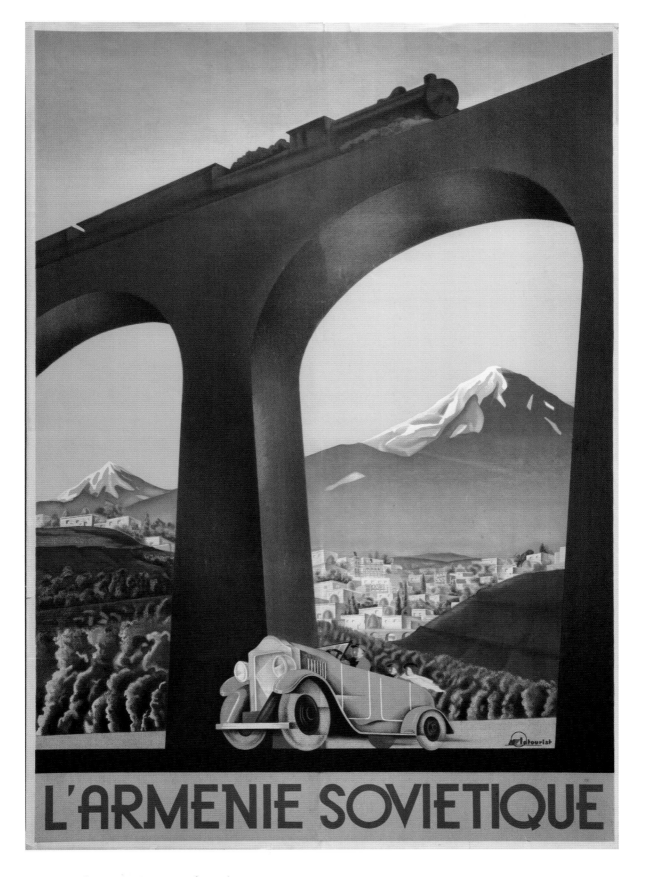

ABOVE: Another Intourist poster from the 1930s –
a testament to the universal language of advertising.

Keep Smiling Through

Between 1939 and 1945, many countries were dragged into a conflagration that consumed every vital resource. Consequently World War II rendered the tourism industry virtually non-existent. Even if civilians were free to travel, petrol rationing in Europe meant holidays were out of the question. 'Putting a brave face on it' became the mantra of the time.

American tourists were once more restricted to holidaying on their own shores. President Franklin D. Roosevelt defined home-grown tourism as a defence of democracy and a patriotic act. But there was little opportunity for vacationing after 1941, when the bombing of Pearl Harbor drew the United States into the war.

After 1945, with much of Europe in ruins, holidays were still far from people's minds. But across the Atlantic the recovery was underway; Americans took to the road, tourism boomed, new attractions opened and ski resorts flourished.

RIGHT: A 1940 London & North Eastern Railway poster by J. Greenup. During the interwar years, as more workers gained annual leave entitlement, massive investment programmes were launched at holiday resorts. The idea of the holiday camp, providing people with all the delights and fun of the seaside on a single site, became enormously popular.

ILLUSTRATED BO

JARROLD & SONS, LTD NORWICH & LONDON

TLIN'S HOLIDAY CAMP
ACTON-ON-SEA
IT'S QUICKER BY RAIL
REE FROM R. P. BUTLIN'S PUBLICITY DEPARTMENT, SKEGNESS, OR ANY L·N·E·R OFFICE OR AGENCY

Printed in Great Britain

Published by the LONDON & NORTH EASTERN RAILWAY

FACING PAGE: During the 1940s American airlines reported an increase in recreational travel. The resulting battle for the skies produced a flood of advertising.

ABOVE: By the 1940s, US railroad companies were struggling to compete with domestic airlines, which offered a cheap, fast service to popular resorts such as Miami Beach and the Bahamas. This Pennsylvania Railroad poster emphasizes the fun to be had in fashionable yet accessible Atlantic City – the 'World's Favorite Playground'.

FACING PAGE: A 1945 United Air Lines poster shows a tourist couple on a cliff overlooking the grandeur of Yosemite Falls and Yosemite National Park while a plane flies overhead.

ABOVE: A 1948 Pan Am poster for flights to the Caribbean references the region's colonial past and reflects cultural attitudes of the period.

ABOVE: The proximity of Mexico to the United States made it a convenient holiday destination where tourists could experience the customs and atmosphere of another country at reasonable expense.

RIGHT: A vigorous campaign encouraging visitors to Mexico was started during the administration of President Avila Comacho (1940–46). The depiction of indigenous people may seem crude to modern eyes, but was widespread at the time.

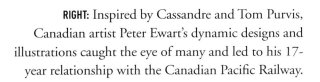

ABOVE: One of the largest railways in the United States became the subject of a popular song, *On the Atchison, Topeka and the Santa Fe*, written by Harry Warren and Johnny Mercer for the movie *The Harvey Girls* (1946), starring Judy Garland.

RIGHT: Inspired by Cassandre and Tom Purvis, Canadian artist Peter Ewart's dynamic designs and illustrations caught the eye of many and led to his 17-year relationship with the Canadian Pacific Railway.

ABOVE: A poster from 1949 promotes beach holidays at the resort of
Norderney, an East Frisian island off the North Sea coast of Germany.
'Always a wonderful experience', reads the confident strapline.

FACING PAGE: This colourful scene with
two figures in the shade of a balcony
by the sea invites visitors to the Greek
island of Hydra.

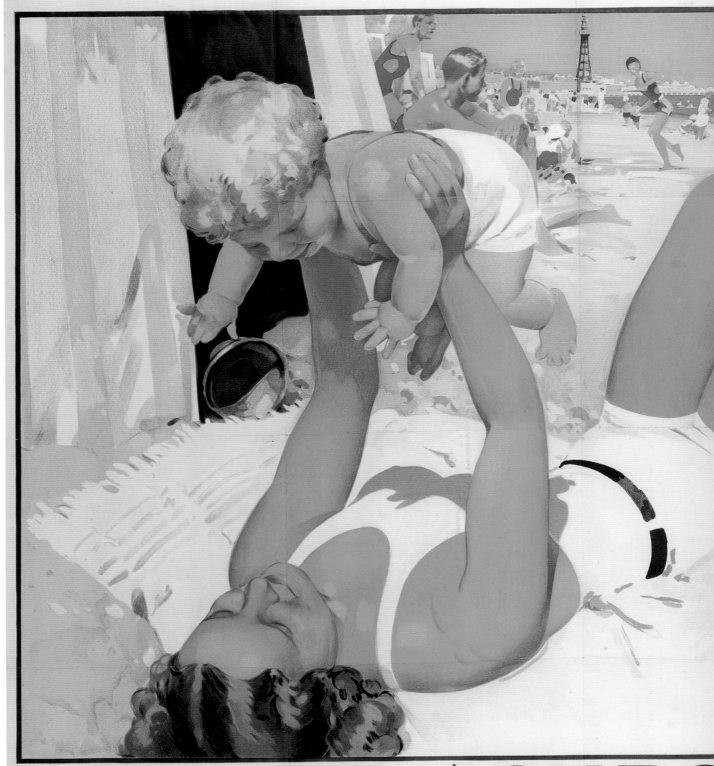

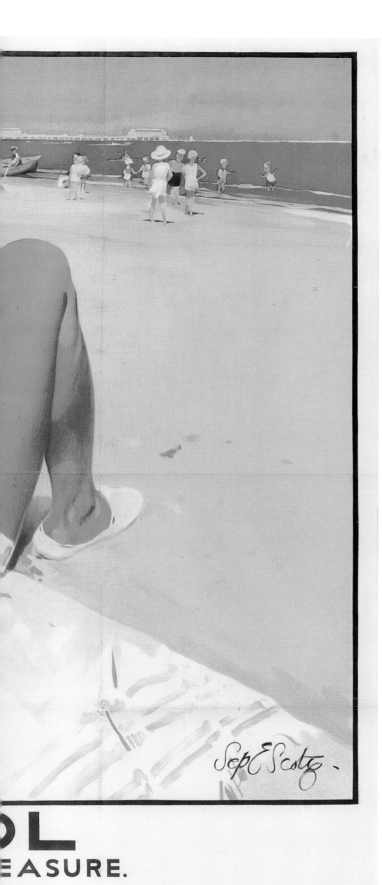

OL

EASURE.

ORT.

LEFT: A London, Midland & Scottish Railway poster by Septimus Scott captures the carefree intimacy of a family beach holiday at the English resort of Blackpool.

Travel Glamour

The mood of the 1950s was coloured by a return to glamour that had been absent during the war years. Back from the conflict, men re-entered the civilian workforce while most women focused on home-making and child-rearing. The conventional family was celebrated; there was a clear demarcation between work and play; and people regarded paid holidays as a basic right.

There was a boom in tourism, largely thanks to economic growth, technological progress and improved transportation and communication networks. An excess of aircraft left over from the war was put to work in the tourist industry. In this new global market, travel companies competed fiercely for customers. Using the new medium of television, holiday operators beamed images of exotic locations direct into people's homes.

ABOVE: In 1953, TCA (later Air Canada) became the first airline in the world to use a computerized reservation system.

FACING PAGE: Although a familiar feature of the 1950s, the presence of a blonde bombshell in this poster raises somewhat unrealistic expectations for the average beach holiday at Exmouth.

EAST COAST

Train services and fares from BRITISH RAILWAYS stations, offices and agencies

PUBLISHED BY THE RAILWAY EXECUTIVE (EASTERN REGION) (A.B. 11/05.)   PRINTED IN GREAT BRITAIN.   JOHN WADDINGTON LTD. LEEDS & LONDON.

ABOVE: This poster promoting rail travel to the east coast of Britain, showing a young couple laughing and splashing in the sea, doubles as a great advert for 1950s swimwear.

FACING PAGE: A voluptuous female fantasy figure is used to entice tourists to Italy's Liguria region.

SANTA·MARGHERITA·LIGURE

ABOVE: A poster for the seaside town of Bangor in Northern Ireland takes its inspiration from contemporary art techniques such as collage and Pop art.

ABOVE: The carnival at Viareggio in northern Italy is a 16-day extravaganza featuring parades, marching bands, floats and street parties. This ENIT poster from 1950 is by local-born graphic artist Uberto Bonetti.

ABOVE: From an era when the night ferry between Britain and France signified
style and class – or a time when such myths were likely to be believed.

ABOVE: A 1955 poster by Fritz Schoppe advertising the East Asia Passenger Service offered by the Hamburg American and North German Lloyd shipping lines.

ABOVE: Commercial artist Bernard Villemot was known for a sharp artistic vision influenced by photography and an ability to distil an advertising message into a memorable image with simple, elegant lines and bold colours.

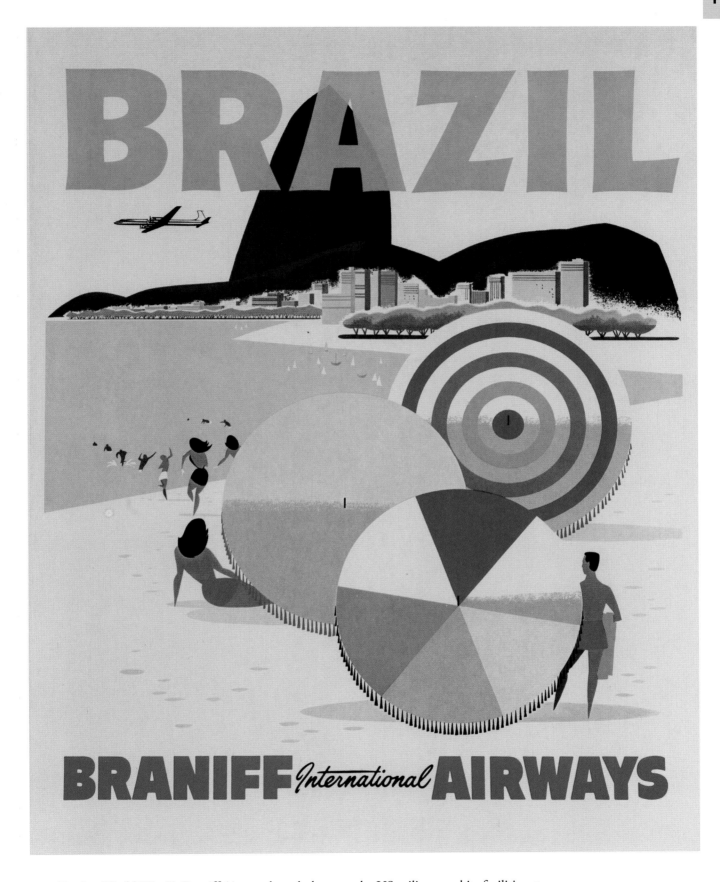

ABOVE: During World War II, Braniff Airways leased planes to the US military and its facilities at Dallas Love Field were used for training pilots and mechanics. After the war the Civil Aeronautics Board awarded Braniff routes to the Caribbean, Central and South America.

ABOVE: The 1950s saw the beginning of a trend for pets in transit – whether as family members or fashion accessories.

FACING PAGE: Surrealism creeps into this poster promoting the resort of New Brighton in northwest England.

RIGHT: A 1957 Danish tourism brochure, with a contemporary art feel.

RIGHT: This 1950s travel poster focuses on Sweden's natural resources, again with a modernist twist.

Northern
SWEDEN

ABOVE: For much of the 20th century, illustrator René Gruau was the hand behind publicity campaigns for many of the world's major fashion houses. His distinctive, sophisticated style – a broad, flowing brushstroke on a ground of flat tone – showed female beauty at its most languorous. Gruau's clients included Dior, Balmain, Schiaparelli and Givenchy. He also did advertising work for companies such as Air France, Omega watches and the French shipping company Chargeurs Réunis.

ABOVE: A modernist treatment of Portuguese traditions and customs from 1954.

Small World

By the 1960s the jet aircraft had replaced the ocean liner as the most glamorous mode of transport. The term 'jet set' was coined to describe an international group of wealthy people who zipped between cities such as Los Angeles, Paris, Rome, London and exclusive retreats on the French and Italian rivieras. To promote the lifestyle, airlines hired cutting-edge commercial artists such as David Klein to produce stylish, glitzy posters.

Back in the real world, a new tourist market opened up as teenagers began to travel abroad *en masse* for the first time. This phenomenon coincided with the increasing universality of the package holiday, which included charter flights, meals, accommodation, guided tours and entertainment. Meanwhile, behind the Iron Curtain, Soviet travel company Intourist continued to offer holidays championing social and technological advances – in stark contrast with the Western consumerist thrills of sun, sea, sex and sangria.

LEFT: This Intourist poster from 1963 highlights the USSR's triumphs in the Space Race.

RIGHT: A 1962 American Pop-art-style poster advertising the Santa Fe Railway.

RIGHT AND FACING PAGE: David Klein designed and illustrated dozens of posters for Howard Hughes' Trans World Airlines (TWA) during the 1950s and 1960s. In many of them he used bright colours and shapes in an abstract style to depict famous landmarks and scenes of cities drawn from the American collective consciousness. His posters came to represent the glow of post-war air travel, the aspirational jet-set style so representative of that era. Like many other poster artists, Klein started his career as a painter and illustrator. In the 1930s, he was part of the California Watercolor Society, a group of artists who got noticed for their original use of paper and colour and their focus on everyday life in California. Their style was characterized by rich colours and free, broad brushstrokes directly applied onto the paper without any preliminary drawings.

ABOVE: A poster for TWA's major rival Pan Am features
a hula skirt illustration made of cut paper.

ABOVE: Another David Klein poster, c.1967, this time for flights to Egypt.

ABOVE: During the 1960s, for the first time, tourism in Hawaii overtook the sugar and pineapple industries in the amount of revenue earned.

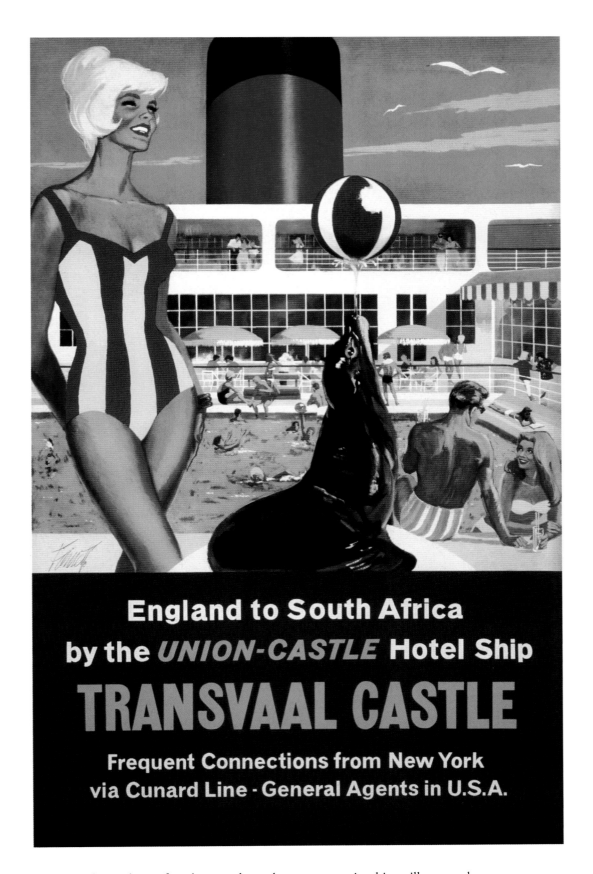

**England to South Africa
by the *UNION-CASTLE* Hotel Ship
TRANSVAAL CASTLE**
Frequent Connections from New York
via Cunard Line - General Agents in U.S.A.

ABOVE: For those who preferred to travel at a slower pace, cruise ships still operated regularly from major ports. The Union-Castle Line was a British company that continued to run until 1977.

Cross with us
to the Continent

BRITISH AND FRENCH RAILWAYS
CAR FERRIES
FROM DOVER TO BOULOGNE & CALAIS

FULL DETAILS OF THESE AND THE DUNKERQUE SERVICE FROM A.A., R.A.C., ANY TRAVEL AGENT
OR CONTINENTAL CAR FERRY CENTRE, 52, GROSVENOR GARDENS, LONDON, S.W.1. TEL. SLOANE 3440

FACING PAGE: A British
Railways poster from 1962.

ABOVE: A British and French Railways poster from 1963 promotes travel
to the continent via car ferries from Dover to Boulogne and Calais.

ABOVE: From a series of colourful, stylized posters for British
Overseas Airways, c.1962.

Printed in U.S.A. P-179

ABOVE: By an unknown artist, the image and typography of this poster showing a mod girl with Union Jack eyes and Pan Am logo mole are quintessential British Swinging Sixties. The message? Be there or be square.

Picture Credits

BRIDGEMAN IMAGES: 7 (The Passenger in Cabin 54 – Yachting, 1896, Toulouse-Lautrec, Henri de (1864-1901) / San Diego Museum of Art, USA / gift of the Baldwin M. Baldwin Foundation); **13,** left (poster advertising the elevator of Notre-Dame de la Garde, Marseilles, c.1900, French School / Private Collection), **13,** right (poster advertising the German East Africa Line, Hamburg, 1904, Stoewer (Stower) Willy (1864-1931) / Cauer Collection, Germany); **14** (poster advertising Cycles Terrot, printed by P. Vercasson, Paris, c.1900, French School, (19th century) / Private Collection / DaTo Images); **15** (poster advertising trains to Monte Carlo, Monaco, 1897, Mucha, Alphonse Marie (1860-1939) / Mucha Trust); **16-17** (poster advertising 'American Line, New York to Southampton', 1905, Cassiers, Hendrick (1858-1944) / Private Collection / The Stapleton Collection); **18** ('Mediterranean, Egypt and the Holy Land', poster advertising the Hamburg American Line, 1909, German School, (20th century) / Cauer Collection, Germany); **25** ('Around the World in 110 Days', poster advertising the Hamburg American Line, 1912 / Cauer Collection, Germany); **37** (poster advertising 'Cunard' routes to Canada, c.1919, English School, (20th century) / Private Collection / DaTo Images); **48** ('What to See in Austria', Austrian School, (20th century) / Private Collection / The Stapleton Collection); **49** (American aviation poster, 1928, American School, (20th century) / Private Collection / Peter Newark American Pictures); **53** ('Live In Kent And Be Content', poster advertising Southern Electric Railways, 1926, White, Ethelbert (1891-1972) / Private Collection / photo © Christie's Images); **59** (poster advertising winter sports in Italy, printed by Levi Cortina, Bozzetto, F. Lenhart, c.1938, Italian School, (20th century) / Private Collection / DaTo Images); **63** (Japan, advertisement for Japanese Government Railways, 1937, Satomi, Munetsugu (1900-95) / Private Collection / DaTo Images); **73** ('North Country Cruises in Summer', poster advertising the Hamburg Southern Line, 1935, Anton, Ottomar (1895-1976) / Cauer Collection, Germany); **75** ('North Country Trips', poster advertising the Hamburg American Line, 1936, Fuss, Albert (1889-1969) / Cauer Collection, Germany); **77** (Dover, poster advertising Southern Railway, 1931, Richmond, Leonard (1889-1965) / Private Collection / photo © Christie's Images); **78** (advertisement for the Holland America Line, c.1932, Hoff (fl.1930s) / Private Collection / DaTo Images); **79** (advertisement for Tyrol, c.1937, Zelger, Arthur (1914-2004) / Private Collection / DaTo Images); **80** ('Canadian Pacific, Happy Cruises', 1937, Purvis, Tom (1888-1959) /Private Collection / photo © Christie's Images); **82** (poster advertising the Spring Festival in Seville, printed by Ortega, Valencia, 1933, Estela (fl.1932) / Private Collection / DaTo Images); **85** (poster of Denmark, printed by Winter & Winter, Danemark, 1939, Refn, Helge (1908-85) / Private Collection / DaTo Images); **91** (TWA poster – Direct to the Southwest, 1941, Walther, Gene (1910-68) / Private Collection / photo © Barbara Singer); **93** (poster advertising 'Pan American World Airlines', c.1948, Arenburg, Mark von (fl.1948) / Private Collection / DaTo Images); **98-99** (Blackpool, Scott, Septimus Edwin (1879-1965) / Private Collection / photo © Christie's Images); **101** (Exmouth, poster advertising British Railways, 1958, Fish, Laurence (1919-2009) / Private Collection / photo © Christie's Images); **104** (Bangor, Hass, Derrick (20th century) / Private Collection / photo © Christie's Images); **107** ('East Asia Passenger Service', poster advertising the Hamburg American Line and the North German Lloyd Line, 1955, Schoppe, Fritz (fl.1955) / Cauer Collection, Germany); **114** ('Relax', an advertising poster for the shipping company Chargeurs Réunis, c.1950, Gruau, René (1909-2004 / Private Collection / photo © Christie's Images); **116** (Visit the USSR, 1963, Russian School, (20th century) / Private Collection / DaTo Images); **117** (poster advertising Santa Fe Railway, transport to Southern California, c.1963, American School, (20th century) / Private Collection / DaTo Images); **121** (poster advertising Trans World Airlines flights to Egypt, c.1967, American School, (20th century) / Private Collection / DaTo Images); **122** (Hawaii, c.1965, American School, (20th century) / Private Collection / DaTo Images); **126** (poster advertising British Overseas Airways, c.1962, English School, (20th century) / Private Collection / DaTo Images)

CORBIS: 23 (© Swim Ink 2, LLC); **29** (© Chris Hellier); **42** (© David Pollack); **54** (© David Pollack); **60** (© Christie's Images); **61** (© Duffy Graphics LLC); **68** (© David Pollack); **69** (© GraphicaArtis); **74** (© Swim Ink 2, LLC); **81** (© Smithsonian Institution); **103** (© GraphicaArtis); **108** (© David Pollack); **109** (© David Pollack); **118** (© David Pollack/K.J. Historical); **119** (© David Pollack); **120** (© David Pollack); **127** (© David Pollack)

MARY EVANS PICTURE LIBRARY: 11 (National Archives, London, England); **30** (Library of Congress); **34** (Retrograph Collection); **55** (Onslow Auctions Limited); **97** (Onslow Auctions Limited); **113** (Onslow Auctions Limited); **123** (Onslow Auctions Limited)

GETTY IMAGES: 12 (Lucien Baylac); **24** (English School); **44** (The LIFE Images Collection); **76; 83** (De Agostini); **102** (Science & Society Picture Library); **112**

SCIENCE & SOCIETY PICTURE LIBRARY: 10 (© NRM/Pictorial Collection); **21** (© Science Museum); **27** (© Science Museum); **36** (© NRM/Pictorial Collection); **38** (© NRM/Pictorial Collection); **46** (© Science Museum); **47** (© NRM/Pictorial Collection); **89** (© NRM/Pictorial Collection); **106** (© NRM/Pictorial Collection); **110** (© NRM/Pictorial Collection); **111** (© NRM/Pictorial Collection); **124** (© NRM/Pictorial Collection); **125** (© NRM/Pictorial Collection)

TOPFOTO: 19 (The Granger Collection); **20** (The Granger Collection); **22** (The Granger Collection); **31** (Ullsteinbild); **35** (The Granger Collection); **45** (The Granger Collection); **50** (The Granger Collection); **52** (City of London/Heritage Images; **86** (Fine Art Images/Heritage Images); **87** (Fine Art Images/Heritage Images)

We have made every attempt to contact the copyright holders of the illustrations within this book. Any oversights or omissions will be corrected in future editions.